UNDERSTANDING
ZEPHANIAH

A Commentary on the Book of Zephaniah using Ancient Bible Study Methods - UPDATED

Michael Harvey Koplitz

CONTENTS

ACKNOWLEDGMENTS

This work could not have been accomplished without Dr. Anne Davis, who taught me Ancient (Hebraic) Bible study methods, and my two study partners, Rev. Dr. Robert Cook and Pastor Sandra Koplitz. We know the journey has just started and will last a lifetime. The discovery of the depths of God's Word is awaiting us to find.

Introduction

While I was attending Seminary earning my M. Div. degree, I questioned what the instructors and reference books, which were required, were saying about the Scriptures. One idea being offered then was that the Bible was full of errors and not factual. I found that attitude disturbing for seminary instructors to be teaching. After all, the Seminary experience is to train pastors to go out into God's world and preach the Bible. How can you preach the Bible if you believe what these instructors are teaching? The methods that were being taught to examine the Bible just seemed inaccurate to me.

After graduating from Seminary, I spent a lot of time reading different views about the Bible. I eventually reached the Zohar. This collection of midrashim are considered the secret work of the Torah, according to Kabbalists. In addition, I read quite a bit about Messianic Judaism. Their view of the Bible is quite different from the seminary view.

I decided that the biblical interpretation that was being taught in Seminary was not the biblical interpretation the people heard when Jesus Christ (whose Hebraic name is Yeshua) preached. I went on a quest to learn what the people of Yeshua's day heard, and what they thought when the Scriptures were read. This quest led me to Dr. Anne Davis and The Bible Learning University. Dr. Davis was in search of the same thing I was searching for. She had made numerous discoveries that helped me in my quest. I earned the Ph.D. degree from The Bible Learning University in Hebraic Studies in Christianity concentrating on ancient Bible Studies methods.

Finally, I found someone who believed that the church has placed almost 1900 years of their theological ideas about the Scriptures, which differed from the original Hebraic thoughts, and in many places, possibly misinterpreted its original meaning. What is also important to hear is that the basic tenants of Yeshua as God's Messiah, my LORD and Savior are in the Bible. My faith in Yeshua is stronger now that I have learned from Dr. Davis how to study the Scriptures in the same manner that the people did in Yeshua's day.

I have included some articles that describe the differences between Greek learning methods and Hebraic learning methods. Please do not skip by them as irrelevant, unless you are familiar with ancient Bible student method, because if you do then the analysis and commentary that follows may become difficult to understand.

Our God is vast and infinite and so is His Word. May God bless you in your discovery of what God's Word is about.

Zephaniah was a prophet sent by the LORD to Judah during the reign of Josiah, after the reformation and cleaning of the Temple in Jerusalem in 621 BCE. In chapter two, verse thirteen Zephaniah tells us that the LORD was about to destroy Nineveh, which was the capital of the Assyrian empire. This assists in the dating of this prophecy.

The subject of this book is God's retribution and the great day of the LORD when God's anger would be poured out against the nations of the Earth because of their sins, which included Judah. Religiously this was the worst period in Judean history for idolatry and desecrations of the Temple in Jerusalem

The immoral worship of Baal and pagan idols were all over the city of Jerusalem. The LORD's answer to these outrages was to send the Babylonian army from the north to destroy Judah and Jerusalem. In the book Zephaniah equates Jerusalem to Nineveh.

In the Eastern Aramaic Peshitta text (translated by George Lamsa) Zephaniah calls the city of Nineveh the city of Jonah. "Oh, the famous city, the saved city; the city of Jonah! She obeyed not the voice; she received not discipline; she trusted not in the Lord; she drew no near to God" (Zephaniah 3:1-2, Eastern Aramaic Peshitta text). [1]

---

[1] Errico, Rocco A., and George M. Lamsa. *Aramaic Light on Ezekiel, Daniel, and the Minor Prophets: A Commentary Based on the Aramaic Language and Ancient Near Eastern Customs.* p. 205.

Zephaniah exhorts the people to repent and gives them assurance to the faithful remnant who will survive the exile.

The Main Difference between the Greek Method and Hebraic Method of Teaching

Once you are aware of the two teaching styles, you will be able to determine if you are in a class or reading a book, whether the analysis and/or teaching method is either in a Greek or Hebraic method. In the Greek method, it is automatically thought that the instructor is right because of advanced knowledge. In the college situation, it is because the professor has his/her Ph.D. in some area of study, so one assumes that he or she knows everything about the topic. For example, Rodney Dangerfield played the role of a middle-aged man going to college. His English midterm was to write about Kurt Vonnegut Jr. Since he didn't understand any of Vonnegut's books, he hired Vonnegut himself to write the midterm. When it was returned to him, the English Professor told Dangerfield that whoever wrote the paper knew nothing about Vonnegut. This is an example of the Greek method of teaching. Did the

Ph.D. English professor think that she knew more about Vonnegut's writings than Vonnegut did?[2]

In the Greek teaching method, the professor or the instructor claims to be the authority. If you are attending a Bible study class and the class leader says, "I will teach you the only way to understand this biblical book," consider the implications. This method is common since most seminaries and Bible colleges teach a Greek method of learning, which is the same method the church has been using for centuries.

Hebraic teaching methods are unique. The teacher wants the students to challenge what they hear. It is through questioning that a student can learn. In addition, the teacher wants his/her students to excel to a point where the student becomes the teacher.
It is said that if two rabbis come together to discuss a passage of Scripture, the result will be at least ten different opinions. All points of view are acceptable if

---

[2] *Back to School.* Performed by Rodney Dangerfield. Hollywood: CA: Paper Clip Productions, 1986. DVD.

biblical evidence can support the points. It is permissible and encourages students to have multiple opinions. There is a depth to God's Word, and God wants us to find all His messages that are placed in the Scriptures.

Seeking the meaning of the Scriptures beyond the literal meaning is essential to fully understanding God's Word.[3] The Greek method of learning the Scriptures has prevailed over the centuries. One problem is that only the literal interpretation of Scripture was often viewed as valid, as prompted by Martin Luther's "sola literalis" meaning that only the literal interpretation of Scripture was valid. The Fundamentalist movements of today are based on the literal interpretation of the Scripture. Therefore, they do not believe that God placed any deeper, hidden, or secret meanings in the Word.

---

[3] Davis, Anne Kimball. *The Synoptic Gospels*. MP3. Albuquerque: NM: BibleInteract, 2012.

The students of the Scriptures who learn through Hebraic training and understanding have drawn a different conclusion. The Hebrew language itself leads to different interpretations because of the construction of the language. The Hebraic method of Bible study opens avenues of thought about God's revelations in the Scripture that may have never been considered. A question may be raised about the Scripture being studied for which there may not be an immediate answer. If so, it becomes the responsibility of the learners to uncover the meaning. Also, remember that multiple opinions about the meaning of Scripture are also acceptable if they can be supported by Scripture.

Methodology

The method employed is to use First Century Scripture study methods integrated with the customs and culture of Yeshua's day to examine the Hebrew and Christian Scriptures, thus gathering a deeper understanding by learning the Scriptures in the way the people of Yeshua's day did.

In typical Rabbinic tradition, I had two study partners. Each one served a different function by looking at the research as I put it together. Rev. Dr. Robert Cook, D. Min., an ordained Elder in the United Methodist Church, has been a study partner in different areas of theology and church leadership. He became interested in Hebraic studies when I started sharing Zohar and Midrash with him. He also completed the entire Disciple program as a student and teacher. My second study partner is my wife, Sandra Koplitz, MS. Sandy and I took the instruction class on teaching the Disciple Bible study program and she takes part in the Zohar study group. Sandy is a licensed local pastor in the United Methodist Church.

The Process of Discovery

I have titled the method of analyzing a passage of Scripture in a Hebraic manner the "Process of Discovery." The author bringing together the various areas of linguistic and cultural understanding, developed this method. There are several sections to the process, and not all the sections apply to every passage of Scripture. The overall result of developing this process is to give the reader a framework into the ideas being presented.

The "Process of Discovery" starts with a Scripture passage. If the passage is in a poetic form, it is identified. Possible poetic techniques include parallelism, chiastic structures, and repetition. Formatting the passage in its poetic form allows the reader to visualize what the first century CE listener was hearing. Any parallelism is shown with colored text and the chiasms are labeled by their corresponding sections, for example: A, B, C, B', A'. Not all passages of the Scriptures have a poetic form.

The next step is to "question the narrative," which is accomplished by assuming the reader knows nothing about the passage. Therefore, the questions go from the simple to the complex. The next task is to identify any linguistic patterns. Linguistic patterns include, but are not limited to: irony, simile, metaphor, symbolism, idioms, hyperbole, figurative language, personification, and allegory.

Any translation inconsistencies discovered between the English NASB version and either the Hebrew or Greek versions are identified. Sometimes a Hebrew or Greek word can be translated in more than one way. Inconsistencies also can be created by the translation committee, which may have used traditional language instead of the actual translation. The decision of the translation committee can be found in the Preface or Introduction to the Bible. Perhaps some inconsistencies were intentionally added to convey some deeper meaning therefore, the inconsistencies need to be examined.

Echoes of the Hebrew Scriptures in the Christian Scripture are identified. This occurs when a passage from the Hebrew Scripture is used in the Christian Scripture or when a Mitzvah is directly discussed in the Christian Scriptures.[4] In addition, echoes can be found when Torah (Genesis through Deuteronomy) passages are used in other Hebrew Bible books. Besides echoes, cross-references are listed. A cross reference is a reference to another verse in the Scripture which can assist the reader to understand the verse that is being read.

The names of people mentioned in the passage are listed. Many of the Hebrew names have meaning and may be associated with places or actions. Jewish parents used to name their children based on what they felt God had in store for their child. An example of this is Abraham whose original name was Abram and was changed to mean eternal father (in this case Abram's name was changed by God to Abraham indicating a

---

[4] Mitzvot are the 613 commandments found in the Torah that please God. There are positive and negative commandments. The list was first development by Maimonides. The full list can be found at: ttp://www.jewfaq.org/613.htm.

function he was to perform). When the Hebrew Bible gives names, many of the occurrences will indicate something special to the reader/listener. The same importance can hold true for the names of places. The time it takes to travel between places can supply insight into the event.

Key words are identified in a verse when they are important to an understanding of that passage. There are no rules for selecting the key words. Searching for other occurrences of the keywords in Scripture in a concordance is necessary to understand how the word was being used; this must be done in either Hebrew or Greek, not in English. A classic Hebraic approach is to find the usage of a word in the Scripture by finding other verses that contain the word. The usage of a word, in its original language, is discovered by searching the Scripture in the language of the Scripture. The verses that contain the word being researched are identified and a pattern for the usage of the word is discerned. Each verse is examined to see what the usage of the word is which, may reveal a pattern for the word's usage. For Hebrew words the first usage of the word in the Scripture, especially if used in the Torah, is important. For the Greek words, the Christian Scriptures are used to determining the word usage in the Scripture. Sometimes finding the equivalent Greek word in the Septuagint and then analyzing its usage in Hebrew can be very helpful.

The Rules of Hillel for Bible understanding can be used when applicable. Hillel was a Torah scholar who lived shortly before Yeshua's day. Hillel developed several rules for Torah students to interpret the Scriptures which are referred to as halachic midrash. In several cases, these rules are helpful in the analysis of the Scripture.

After the linguistic analysis is complete, an examination of the cultural implications will be examined. The culture is important because it is not specifically referenced in the biblical narratives as shown earlier. From the linguistic analysis and the cultural understanding, it is possible to get a deeper meaning of the Scripture beyond the literal meaning of the plaintext. That is what the listeners of Yeshua's time were doing. They put linguistics and the culture together without even having to contemplate it. They simply did it.

This will lead to a conclusion or a set of conclusions about what the passage is talking about. Most of the time, the Hebraic analysis leads to the desire for a deeper analysis to fully understand what Yeshua was talking about or what was happening to Him. Whatever the result, a new deeper understanding of the Scripture will be obtained.

The components of the Process of Discovery are:
Linguistics Section

      Linguistic Structure of the Scripture

      Discussion

      Questioning the Passage

      Main/Center Point

      Verse Comparison on citations or proof text

      Idioms

      Metaphors

      Symbols

Translation inconsistencies

People's names

Name of places

Word Study

Scripture cross references

Echoes

Rules of Hillel

Culture Section

Discussion

Questioning the passage culturally

Culture and Linguistics Section

Discussion

Only the sections pertinent to each chapter of Jonah
are included.

Zephaniah Chapter One

Language

New American Standard 1995	Hebrew	Septuagint
The word of the LORD which came to Zephaniah son of Cushi, son of Gedaliah, son of Amariah, son of Hezekiah, in the days of Josiah son of Amon, king of Judah: 2 "I will completely remove all *things* From the face of the earth," declares the LORD. 3 "I will remove man and beast; I will remove the birds of the sky And the fish of the sea, And the ruins along with the wicked; And I will cut off man from the face of the earth," declares the LORD.	דְּבַר־יְהוָה| אֲשֶׁר הָיָה אֶל־צְפַנְיָה בֶּן־כּוּשִׁי בֶּן־גְּדַלְיָה בֶּן־אֲמַרְיָה בֶּן־חִזְקִיָּה בִּימֵי יֹאשִׁיָּהוּ בֶן־אָמֹון מֶלֶךְ יְהוּדָה: 2 אָסֹף אָסֵף כֹּל מֵעַל פְּנֵי הָאֲדָמָה נְאֻם־יְהוָה: 3 אָסֵף אָדָם וּבְהֵמָה אָסֵף עוֹף־הַשָּׁמַיִם וּדְגֵי הַיָּם וְהַמַּכְשֵׁלוֹת אֶת־הָרְשָׁעִים וְהִכְרַתִּי אֶת־הָאָדָם מֵעַל פְּנֵי הָאֲדָמָה נְאֻם־יְהוָה: 4 וְנָטִיתִי יָדִי עַל־יְהוּדָה וְעַל כָּל־יוֹשְׁבֵי יְרוּשָׁלָ͏ִם וְהִכְרַתִּי מִן־הַמָּקוֹם הַזֶּה אֶת־שְׁאָר הַבַּעַל אֶת־שֵׁם הַכְּמָרִים עִם־הַכֹּהֲנִים:	The word of the Lord which came to Sophonias the son of Chusi, the son of Godolias, the son of Amorias, the son of Ezekias, in the days of Josias son of Amon, king of Juda. 2 Let there be an utter cutting off from the face of the land, saith the Lord. 3 Let man and cattle be cut off; let the birds of the air and the fishes of the sea be cut off; and the ungodly shall fail, and I will take away the transgressors from the face of the land, saith the Lord. 4 And I will stretch out mine hand upon Juda, and

4 "So I will stretch out My hand against Judah And against all the inhabitants of Jerusalem. And I will cut off the remnant of Baal from this place, *And* the names of the idolatrous priests along with the priests.

5 "And those who bow down on the housetops to the host of heaven, And those who bow down *and* swear to the LORD and *yet* swear by Milcom,

6 And those who have turned back from following the LORD, And those who have not sought the LORD or inquired of Him."

7 Be silent before the Lord GOD! For the day of the LORD is near, For the LORD has prepared a sacrifice, He has consecrated His guests.

8 "Then it will come about on the

5 וְאֶת־הַמִּשְׁתַּחֲוִים עַל־הַגַּגּוֹת לִצְבָא הַשָּׁמָיִם וְאֶת־הַמִּשְׁתַּחֲוִים הַנִּשְׁבָּעִים לַיהֹוָה וְהַנִּשְׁבָּעִים בְּמַלְכָּם:

6 וְאֶת־הַנְּסוֹגִים מֵאַחֲרֵי יְהֹוָה וַאֲשֶׁר לֹא־בִקְשׁוּ אֶת־יְהֹוָה וְלֹא דְרָשֻׁהוּ:

7 הַס מִפְּנֵי אֲדֹנָי יְהֹוָה כִּי קָרוֹב יוֹם יְהֹוָה כִּי־הֵכִין יְהֹוָה זֶבַח הִקְדִּישׁ קְרֻאָיו:

8 וְהָיָה בְּיוֹם זֶבַח יְהֹוָה וּפָקַדְתִּי עַל־הַשָּׂרִים וְעַל־בְּנֵי הַמֶּלֶךְ וְעַל כָּל־הַלֹּבְשִׁים מַלְבּוּשׁ נָכְרִי:

9 וּפָקַדְתִּי עַל כָּל־הַדּוֹלֵג עַל־הַמִּפְתָּן בַּיּוֹם הַהוּא הַמְמַלְאִים בֵּית אֲדֹנֵיהֶם חָמָס וּמִרְמָה: ס

10 וְהָיָה בַיּוֹם הַהוּא נְאֻם־יְהֹוָה קוֹל צְעָקָה מִשַּׁעַר הַדָּגִים וִילָלָה מִן־הַמִּשְׁנֶה וְשֶׁבֶר גָּדוֹל מֵהַגְּבָעוֹת:

upon all the inhabitants of Jerusalem; and I will remove the names of Baal out of this place, and the names of the priests;

5 and them that worship the host of heaven upon the house-tops; and them that worship and swear by the Lord, and them that swear by their king;

6 and them that turn aside from the Lord, and them that seek not the Lord, and them that cleave not to the Lord.

7 Fear ye before the Lord God; for the day of the Lord is near; for the Lord has prepared his sacrifice, and has sanctified his guests.

8 And it shall come to pass in the day of the Lord's sacrifice, that I will take vengeance on the princes, and on the king's house, and upon all that

day of the LORD'S sacrifice That I will punish the princes, the king's sons And all who clothe themselves with foreign garments.

9 "And I will punish on that day all who leap on the *temple* threshold, Who fill the house of their lord with violence and deceit.

10 "On that day," declares the LORD, "There will be the sound of a cry from the Fish Gate, A wail from the Second Quarter, And a loud crash from the hills.

11 "Wail, O inhabitants of the Mortar, For all the people of Canaan will be silenced; All who weigh out silver will be cut off.

12 "It will come about at that time That I will search Jerusalem with lamps, And I will punish the men Who are stagnant

11 הֵילִ֙ילוּ֙ יֹשְׁבֵ֣י הַמַּכְתֵּ֔שׁ כִּ֥י נִדְמָ֖ה כָּל־עַ֣ם כְּנַ֑עַן נִכְרְת֖וּ כָּל־נְטִ֥ילֵי כָֽסֶף׃

12 וְהָיָה֙ בָּעֵ֣ת הַהִ֔יא אֲחַפֵּ֥שׂ אֶת־יְרוּשָׁלַ֖͏ִם בַּנֵּר֑וֹת וּפָקַדְתִּ֣י עַל־הָאֲנָשִׁ֗ים הַקֹּֽפְאִים֙ עַל־שִׁמְרֵיהֶ֔ם הָאֹֽמְרִים֙ בִּלְבָבָ֔ם לֹֽא־יֵיטִ֥יב יְהוָ֖ה וְלֹ֥א יָרֵֽעַ׃

13 וְהָיָ֤ה חֵילָם֙ לִמְשִׁסָּ֔ה וּבָתֵּיהֶ֖ם לִשְׁמָמָ֑ה וּבָנ֤וּ בָתִּים֙ וְלֹ֣א יֵשֵׁ֔בוּ וְנָטְע֣וּ כְרָמִ֔ים וְלֹ֥א יִשְׁתּ֖וּ אֶת־יֵינָֽם׃

14 קָר֤וֹב יוֹם־יְהוָה֙ הַגָּד֔וֹל קָר֖וֹב וּמַהֵ֣ר מְאֹ֑ד ק֚וֹל י֣וֹם יְהוָ֔ה מַ֥ר צֹרֵ֖חַ שָׁ֥ם גִּבּֽוֹר׃

15 י֥וֹם עֶבְרָ֖ה הַיּ֣וֹם הַה֑וּא י֧וֹם צָרָ֣ה וּמְצוּקָ֗ה י֤וֹם שֹׁאָה֙ וּמְשׁוֹאָ֔ה י֥וֹם חֹ֙שֶׁךְ֙ וַאֲפֵלָ֔ה י֥וֹם עָנָ֖ן וַעֲרָפֶֽל׃

16 י֥וֹם שׁוֹפָ֖ר וּתְרוּעָ֑ה עַ֚ל הֶעָרִ֣ים הַבְּצֻר֔וֹת

wear strange apparel.

9 And I will openly take vengeance on the porches in that day, *on the men* that fill the house of the Lord their God with ungodliness and deceit.

10 And there shall be in that day, saith the Lord, the sound of a cry from the gate of men slaying, and a howling from the second *gate*, and a great crashing from the hills.

11 Lament, ye that inhabit the *city* that has been broken down, for all the people has become like Chanaan; and all that were exalted by silver have been utterly destroyed.

12 And it shall come to pass in that day, *that* I will search Jerusalem with a candle, and will take vengeance on the men that despise the things committed to them; but they say in their hearts, The

in spirit, Who say in their hearts, 'The LORD will not do good or evil!'

13 "Moreover, their wealth will become plunder And their houses desolate; Yes, they will build houses but not inhabit *them*, And plant vineyards but not drink their wine."

14 Near is the great day of the LORD, Near and coming very quickly; Listen, the day of the LORD! In it the warrior cries out bitterly.

15 A day of wrath is that day, A day of trouble and distress, A day of destruction and desolation, A day of darkness and gloom, A day of clouds and thick darkness,

16 A day of trumpet and battle cry Against the fortified cities And the high corner towers.

17 I will bring distress on men So

וְעַל הַפִּנּוֹת הַגְּבֹהוֹת:
17 וַהֲצֵרֹתִי לָאָדָם וְהָלְכוּ כַּעִוְרִים כִּי לַיהֹוָה חָטָאוּ וְשֻׁפַּךְ דָּמָם כֶּעָפָר וּלְחֻמָם כַּגְּלָלִים: 18 גַּם־כַּסְפָּם גַּם־זְהָבָם לֹא־יוּכַל לְהַצִּילָם בְּיוֹם עֶבְרַת יְהֹוָה וּבְאֵשׁ קִנְאָתוֹ תֵּאָכֵל כָּל־הָאָרֶץ כִּי־כָלָה אַךְ־נִבְהָלָה יַעֲשֶׂה אֵת כָּל־יֹשְׁבֵי הָאָרֶץ:
ס

Lord will not do any good, neither will he do any evil.

13 And their power shall be for a spoil, and their houses for utter desolation; and they shall build houses, but shall not dwell in them; and they shall plant vineyards, but shall not drink the wine of them.

14 For the great day of the Lord *is* near, *it is* near, and very speedy; the sound of the day of the Lord is made bitter and harsh.

15 A mighty day of wrath is that day, a day of affliction and distress, a day of desolation and destruction, a day of gloominess and darkness, a day of cloud and vapour,

16 a day of the trumpet and cry against the strong cities, and against the high towers.

17 And I will greatly afflict the men, and they shall walk as blind men, because they have

that they will walk like the blind, Because they have sinned against the LORD; And their blood will be poured out like dust And their flesh like dung. [18] Neither their silver nor their gold Will be able to deliver them On the day of the LORD'S wrath; And all the earth will be devoured In the fire of His jealousy, For He will make a complete end, Indeed a terrifying one, Of all the inhabitants of the earth.		sinned against the Lord; therefore he shall pour out their blood as dust, and their flesh as dung. [18] And their silver and their gold shall in nowise be able to rescue them in the day of the Lord's wrath; but the whole land shall be devoured by the fire of his jealously; for he will bring a speedy destruction on all them that inhabit the land.

Process of Discovery

Linguistics Section

Linguistic Structure

[1] The word of the LORD which came to Zephaniah son of Cushi, son of Gedaliah, son of Amariah, son of Hezekiah, in the days of Josiah son of Amon, king of Judah:

A [2] **"I will completely remove all** *things* From the face of the earth," declares the LORD. [3] "I will remove man and beast; I will remove the birds of the sky And the fish of the sea, And the ruins along with the wicked; And I will cut off man from the face of the earth," declares the LORD. [4] "So I will stretch out My hand against Judah And against all the inhabitants of Jerusalem. And I will cut off the remnant of Baal from this place, *And* the names of the idolatrous priests along with the priests. [5] "And those who bow down on the housetops to the host of heaven, And those who bow down *and* swear to the LORD and *yet* swear by Milcom, [6] And those who have turned back from following the LORD, And those who have not sought the LORD or inquired of Him."

B [7] Be silent before the Lord GOD! **For the day of the LORD is near,** For the LORD has prepared a sacrifice, He has consecrated His guests. [8] "Then it will come about on the day of the LORD'S sacrifice That I will punish the princes, the king's sons And all who clothe themselves with foreign garments. [9] "And I will punish on that day all who leap on the *temple* threshold, Who fill the house of their lord with violence and deceit.

C [10] **"On that day,"** declares the LORD, "There will be the sound of a cry from the Fish Gate, A wail from the Second Quarter, And a loud crash from the hills. [11] "Wail, O inhabitants of the Mortar, For all the people of Canaan will be silenced; All who weigh out silver will be cut off.

C' [12] "It will come about **at that time** That I will search Jerusalem with lamps, And I will punish the men Who are stagnant in spirit, Who say in their hearts, 'The LORD will not do good or evil!' [13] "Moreover, their wealth will become plunder And their houses desolate; Yes, they will build houses but not inhabit *them*, And plant vineyards but not drink their wine."

B' [14] Near is the great day of the LORD, Near and coming very quickly; Listen, the day of the LORD! In it the warrior cries out bitterly. [15] A day of wrath is that day, A day of trouble and distress, A day of destruction and desolation, A day of darkness and gloom, A day of clouds and thick darkness, [16] A day of trumpet and battle cry Against the fortified cities And the high corner towers.

A' [17] I will bring distress on men So that they will walk like the blind, Because they have sinned against the LORD; And their blood will be poured out like dust And their flesh like dung. [18] Neither their silver nor their gold Will be able to deliver them On the day of the LORD'S wrath; And **all the earth will be devoured In the fire of His jealousy**, For He will make a complete end, Indeed a terrifying one, Of all the inhabitants of the earth.

Discussion

Chapter one of Zephaniah starts immediately with a decree from the LORD that He intends to destroy all life on the planet. The day this will occur is called the "day of the LORD." On this day, the LORD will physically return to Earth and the final correction (the Tukkin) will occur. The evil and sinful people of the world will be destroyed. The center of the chiasm contains two warnings about the Day of the LORD.

Questioning the Passage

1. The intention of the LORD is repeated in verse two and three. Why the extreme emphasis? God's chosen people seemed to forget that the LORD was the creator and sustainer of life on Earth. The people had turned away from the LORD and to the Baal cult and other pagan religions. Therefore, the LORD wanted to ensure that the people knew exactly where their punishment was coming from.

2. What does it mean to cut off the remnant of the Baal? (v. 4)

   In the judgment that the LORD will execute, He will destroy all that remained of the Baal cult, so that no one will ever worship Baal again.

3. What does it mean when the LORD says that He will stretch His hand against Judah? (v. 4)

   This is an idiom meaning that the LORD was going to proclaim and execute judgment on the people of Judah.

4. Who was Milcom? (v. 5)

   Milcom was a god of the Ammonites.

5. What does it mean to make inquiry of the LORD? (v. 6)

   To make an inquiry of the LORD is to praise the LORD and to turn to the LORD for what one needs to live.

6. What is the LORD's sacrifice? (v. 7)

The LORD's sacrifice would be the death of all the Hebrews who turned away from the LORD to worship the pagan gods of Baal and Milcom.

7. What does it mean that the LORD consecrated his guests? (v. 7)

The Hebrew word *qadash* is translated into the English word "consecrated." It can also be translated as "set apart." The LORD is saying that He will set apart his guests on the day of the LORD. The guests are the wicked people of the day, especially those who have rejected the Torah and who worshiped the pagan gods.

8. What does it mean to leap over the threshold? (v. 9)

The Targum of Zephaniah reads instead of 'the threshold,' it reads "the laws of the Philistines." This verse refers to the people who lived by the laws of the Philistines instead of the Laws of the LORD.

9. Where was the Fish Gate? (v 10)

The Fish gate was the gate into the city of Jerusalem where fish merchants sold their fish. The gate got its name from the activity that occurred at it.[5]

10. Where was the Second Quarter? (v. 10)

This is the area of Jerusalem near the Fish gate.

11. Who were the inhabitants of the Mortar? (v. 11)

It is believed that Mortar was a section of the city of Jerusalem. No evidence remains about this section of the city. It was possibly in a lower elevation of the city which was destroyed by the Babylonians. No artifacts, to date, have been found from this section of the city.

---

[5] Scherman, Nosson, and Meir Zlotowitz. "Zephaniah." *Isaiah: The Later Prophets with a Commentary Antholigized from the Rabbinic Writings.* Brooklyn, N.Y: Mesorah Publications, 2013. N. pag. Print.

12. What is the terrible end to the inhabitants of the Earth? (v. 18)

The Targum says that all life will be exterminated on earth on the Day of the LORD.

Main/Center Point

The Chosen People of God were rebelling against the LORD's Torah. The people turned away from the worship of the LORD and towards the Baal and Milcom cult, which was completely unacceptable. The LORD tells the people of one of their numerous practices that violates the Torah. That violation was the wearing of clothing that was not of the tribe of Judah. Perhaps the people thought that if they did not look like Hebrews, because of their clothing, then the LORD would not see their violation of the Torah.

People's names

1. צְפַנְיָה *Tsephanyah* or צְפַנְיָהוּ *Tsephanyahu* **Meaning:** 'Yah has treasured'

2. גְּדַלְיָה *Gedalyah* **Meaning:** 'Yah is great'

3. אֲמַרְיָהוּ *Amaryahu* or אֲמַרְיָה *Amaryah*

    Meaning: 'Yah has promised,' the name of several Israelites

4. חִזְקִיָּה *Chizqiyyah* or חִזְקִיָּהוּ *Chizqiyyahu* or יְחִזְקִיָּה *Yechizqiyyah* or יְחִזְקִיָּהוּ *Yechizqiyyahu*

    Meaning: 'Yah has strengthened,' a king of Judah, also several other Israelites

5. יֹאשִׁיָּה *Yoshiyyah* or יֹאשִׁיָּהוּ *Yoshiyyahu* **Meaning:** 'Yah supports,' two Israelites

6. אָמוֹן *Amon* **Meaning:** 'masterworkman,' three Israelites

Name of places

1. יְהוּדָה *Yehudah* **Meaning:** 'praised,' a son of Jacob, also his descendants, the Southern kingdom

2. כְּנַעַן *Kenaan* **Meaning:** a son of Ham, also his descendants and their land west of the Jordan

3. מַכְתֵּשׁ *Maktesh* **Meaning:** a place probably in Jerusalem (translated "Mortar").

Culture Section

Questioning the passage

1. What is the rule about dressing in foreign attire? (v. 8)

    In the Near East, the different tribes and nations had their own religions and their own distinct clothing. Until recently, it was unlawful to wear the clothing of another race. This enabled the quick identification of people. In Zephaniah's time, it was sacrilegious to wear the clothing of an alien race or of the members of rival religion.[6]

Thoughts

This chapter reminds us that one day the wrath of the LORD will be brought down upon God's people who ignore the Torah. The LORD sent numerous prophets to warn the people what this would happen if they continued in their pagan ways. The Torah was given to

---

[6] Errico, Rocco A., and George M. Lamsa. "Zephaniah." *Aramaic Light on Ezekiel, Daniel, and the Minor Prophets: A Commentary Based on the Aramaic Language and Ancient Near Eastern Customs.* Smyrna, GA: Noohra Foundation, 2012. N. pag. Print.

the Hebrews to help them live righteously in the LORD's sight. However, in this time before the Babylonian Exile, the people openly violated the Torah. When the Day of the LORD comes, even the rich cannot use their gold and silver to stop the wrath of the LORD. In ancient days, the rich usually became rich by exploiting their brothers and sisters. They violated the Torah, which tells us not to exploit our brothers and sisters. The Day of the LORD will see the end of life upon the Earth. The violators of the Torah are going to see the worst of the LORD's wrath.

Zephaniah Chapter Two

Language

New American Standard 1995	Hebrew	Septuagint
1 Gather yourselves together, yes, gather, O nation without shame, 2 Before the decree takes effect-- The day passes like the chaff-- Before the burning anger of the LORD comes upon you, Before the day of the LORD'S anger comes upon you. 3 Seek the LORD, All you humble of the earth Who have carried out His ordinances; Seek righteousness, seek humility. Perhaps you will be hidden In the day of the LORD'S anger. 4 For Gaza will be abandoned And Ashkelon a desolation; Ashdod will be driven out at noon And Ekron will be uprooted.	הִתְקוֹשְׁשׁוּ¹ וָקוֹשּׁוּ הַגּוֹי לֹא נִכְסָף: בְּטֶרֶם² לֶדֶת חֹק כְּמֹץ עָבַר יוֹם בְּטֶרֶם׀ לֹא־יָבוֹא עֲלֵיכֶם חֲרוֹן׀ אַף־יְהוָה בְּטֶרֶם לֹא־יָבוֹא עֲלֵיכֶם יוֹם אַף־ יְהוָה: ³ בַּקְּשׁוּ אֶת־ יְהוָה כָּל־עַנְוֵי הָאָרֶץ אֲשֶׁר מִשְׁפָּטוֹ פָּעָלוּ בַּקְּשׁוּ־צֶדֶק בַּקְּשׁוּ עֲנָוָה אוּלַי תִּסָּתְרוּ בְּיוֹם אַף־יְהוָה: ⁴ כִּי עַזָּה עֲזוּבָה תִהְיֶה וְאַשְׁקְלוֹן לִשְׁמָמָה אַשְׁדּוֹד בַּצָּהֳרַיִם יְגָרְשׁוּהָ וְעֶקְרוֹן תֵּעָקֵר: ס ⁵ הוֹי יֹשְׁבֵי חֶבֶל הַיָּם גּוֹי כְּרֵתִים	Be ye gathered and closely joined together, O unchastened nation; 2 before ye become as the flower that passes away, before the anger of the Lord come upon you, before the day of the wrath of the Lord come upon you. 3 Seek ye the Lord, all ye meek of the earth; do judgment, and seek justice, and answer accordingly; that ye may be hid in the day of the wrath of the Lord. 4 For Gaza shall be utterly spoiled, and Ascalon shall be destroyed; and Azotus shall be cast forth at

5 Woe to the inhabitants of the seacoast, The nation of the Cherethites! The word of the LORD is against you, O Canaan, land of the Philistines; And I will destroy you So that there will be no inhabitant.

6 So the seacoast will be pastures, *With* caves for shepherds and folds for flocks.

7 And the coast will be For the remnant of the house of Judah, They will pasture on it. In the houses of Ashkelon they will lie down at evening; For the LORD their God will care for them And restore their fortune.

8 "I have heard the taunting of Moab And the revilings of the sons of Ammon, With which they have taunted My people And become arrogant against their territory.

9 "Therefore, as I live," declares the

דְּבַר־יְהֹוָה
עֲלֵיכֶם כְּנַעַן
אֶרֶץ פְּלִשְׁתִּים
וְהַאֲבַדְתִּיךְ מֵאֵין
יוֹשֵׁב:
6 וְהָיְתָה חֶבֶל
הַיָּם נְוֹת כְּרֹת
רֹעִים וְגִדְרוֹת
צֹאן:
7 וְהָיָה חֶבֶל
לִשְׁאֵרִית בֵּית
יְהוּדָה עֲלֵיהֶם
יִרְעוּן בְּבָתֵּי
אַשְׁקְלוֹן בָּעֶרֶב
יִרְבָּצוּן כִּי
יִפְקְדֵם יְהֹוָה
אֱלֹהֵיהֶם וְשָׁב
(שְׁבוּתָם)
[שְׁבִיתָם]:
8 שָׁמַעְתִּי חֶרְפַּת
מוֹאָב וְגִדּוּפֵי בְּנֵי
עַמּוֹן אֲשֶׁר חֵרְפוּ
אֶת־עַמִּי וַיַּגְדִּילוּ
עַל־גְּבוּלָם:
9 לָכֵן חַי־אָנִי
נְאֻם יְהֹוָה
צְבָאוֹת אֱלֹהֵי
יִשְׂרָאֵל כִּי־מוֹאָב
כִּסְדֹם תִּהְיֶה
וּבְנֵי עַמּוֹן
כַּעֲמֹרָה מִמְשַׁק
חָרוּל וּמִכְרֵה־
מֶלַח וּשְׁמָמָה

noon-day, and Accaron shall be rooted up.

5 Woe to them that dwell on the border of the sea, neighbours of the Cretans! the word of the Lord is against you, O Chanaan, land of the Philistines, and I will destroy you out of *your* dwelling-place.

6 And Crete shall be a pasture of flocks, and a fold of sheep.

7 And the sea cost shall be for the remnant of the house of Juda; they shall pasture upon them in the houses of Ascalon; they shall rest in the evening because of the children of Juda; for the Lord their God has visited them, and he will turn away their captivity.

8 I have heard the revilings of Moab, and the insults of the children of Ammon, wherewith they

LORD of hosts, The God of Israel, "Surely Moab will be like Sodom And the sons of Ammon like Gomorrah-- A place possessed by nettles and salt pits, And a perpetual desolation. The remnant of My people will plunder them And the remainder of My nation will inherit them."

10 This they will have in return for their pride, because they have taunted and become arrogant against the people of the LORD of hosts.

11 The LORD will be terrifying to them, for He will starve all the gods of the earth; and all the coastlands of the nations will bow down to Him, everyone from his *own* place.

12 "You also, O Ethiopians, will be slain by My sword."

13 And He will stretch out His hand against the north And destroy

עַד־עוֹלָ֑ם שְׁאֵרִ֤ית עַמִּי֙ יְבָז֔וּם וְיֶ֥תֶר (גּוֹי) [גּוֹיִ֖י] יִנְחָל֥וּם׃ 10 זֹ֥את לָהֶם֙ תַּ֣חַת גְּאוֹנָ֔ם כִּ֤י חֵֽרְפוּ֙ וַיַּגְדִּ֔לוּ עַל־עַ֖ם יְהוָ֥ה צְבָאֽוֹת׃ 11 נוֹרָ֤א יְהוָה֙ עֲלֵיהֶ֔ם כִּ֣י רָזָ֔ה אֵ֖ת כָּל־אֱלֹהֵ֣י הָאָ֑רֶץ וְיִשְׁתַּֽחֲווּ־ל֗וֹ אִ֚ישׁ מִמְּקוֹמ֔וֹ כֹּ֖ל אִיֵּ֥י הַגּוֹיִֽם׃ 12 גַּם־אַתֶּ֣ם כּוּשִׁ֔ים חַֽלְלֵ֥י חַרְבִּ֖י הֵֽמָּה׃ 13 וְיֵ֤ט יָדוֹ֙ עַל־צָפ֔וֹן וִֽיאַבֵּ֖ד אֶת־אַשּׁ֑וּר וְיָשֵׂ֤ם אֶת־נִֽינְוֵה֙ לִשְׁמָמָ֔ה צִיָּ֖ה כַּמִּדְבָּֽר׃ 14 וְרָבְצ֨וּ בְתוֹכָ֜הּ עֲדָרִ֗ים כָּל־חַיְתוֹ־ג֔וֹי גַּם־קָאַת֙ גַּם־קִפֹּ֔ד בְּכַפְתֹּרֶ֖יהָ יָלִ֑ינוּ ק֣וֹל יְשׁוֹרֵ֣ר בַּֽחַלּ֗וֹן חֹ֙רֶב֙ בַּסַּ֔ף כִּ֥י אַרְזָ֖ה עֵרָֽה׃

have reviled my people, and magnified themselves against my coasts.

9 Therefore, *as* I live, saith the Lord of hosts, the God of Israel, Moab shall be as Sodoma, and the children of Ammon as Gomorrha; and Damascus *shall be* left as a heap of the threshing-floor, and desolate for ever: and the remnant of my people shall plunder them, and the remnant of my nations shall inherit them.

10 This is their punishment in return for their haughtiness, because they have reproached and magnified themselves against the Lord Almighty.

11 The Lord shall appear against them, and shall utterly destroy all the gods of the nations of the

Assyria, And He will make Nineveh a desolation, Parched like the wilderness.

14 Flocks will lie down in her midst, All beasts which range in herds; Both the pelican and the hedgehog Will lodge in the tops of her pillars; Birds will sing in the window, Desolation *will be* on the threshold; For He has laid bare the cedar work.

15 This is the exultant city Which dwells securely, Who says in her heart, "I am, and there is no one besides me." How she has become a desolation, A resting place for beasts! Everyone who passes by her will hiss *And* wave his hand *in contempt.*

15 זֹאת הָעִיר הָעַלִּיזָה הַיּוֹשֶׁבֶת לָבֶטַח הָאֹמְרָה בִּלְבָבָהּ אֲנִי וְאַפְסִי עוֹד אֵיךְ הָיְתָה לְשַׁמָּה מַרְבֵּץ לַחַיָּה כֹּל עוֹבֵר עָלֶיהָ יִשְׁרֹק יָנִיעַ יָדוֹ

earth; and they shall worship him every one from his place, *even* all the islands of the nations.

12 Ye Ethiopians also are the slain of my sword.

13 And he shall stretch forth his hand against the north and destroy the Assyrian, and make Nineve a dry wilderness, *even* as a desert.

14 And flocks, and all the wild beasts of the land, and chameleons shall feed in the midst thereof: and hedgehogs shall lodge in the ceilings thereof; and wild beasts shall cry in the breaches thereof, and ravens in her porches, whereas her loftiness was *as* as cedar.

Process of Discovery

Linguistics Section

Linguistic Structure

[Exhortation] [1]Gather yourselves together, yes, gather, O nation without shame, [2] Before the decree takes effect-- The day passes like the chaff-- Before the burning anger of the LORD comes upon you, Before the day of the LORD'S anger comes upon you. [3] Seek the LORD, All you humble of the earth Who have carried out His ordinances; Seek righteousness, seek humility. Perhaps you will be hidden In the day of the LORD'S anger. [4] For Gaza will be abandoned And Ashkelon a desolation; Ashdod will be driven out at noon And Ekron will be uprooted.

A [5] Woe to the inhabitants of the seacoast, The nation of the Cherethites! The word of the LORD is against you, O Canaan, land of the Philistines; And I will destroy you **So that there will be no inhabitant**.

B [6] So the seacoast will be pastures, *With* caves for shepherds and **folds for flocks**. [7] And the coast will be For the remnant of the house of Judah, They will pasture on it. In the houses of Ashkelon they will lie down at evening; For the LORD their God will care for them And restore their fortune.

C [8] "I have heard the taunting of Moab And the revilings of the sons of Ammon, With which they have taunted My people And become arrogant against their territory. [9] "Therefore, as I live," declares the LORD of hosts, The God of Israel, "Surely Moab will be like Sodom And the sons of Ammon like Gomorrah-- A place possessed by nettles and salt pits, **And a perpetual desolation**. The remnant of My people will plunder them And the remainder of My nation will inherit them." [10] This they will have in return for their pride, because they have taunted and become arrogant against the people of the LORD of hosts.

A' [11] The LORD will be terrifying to them, for He will **starve all the gods of the earth**; and all the coastlands of the nations will bow down to Him, everyone from his *own* place. [12] "You also, O Ethiopians, will be slain by My sword." [13] And He will stretch out His hand against the north And destroy Assyria, And He will make Nineveh a desolation, Parched like the wilderness.

    B' [14] **Flocks** will lie down in her midst, All beasts which range in herds; Both the pelican and the hedgehog Will lodge in the tops of her pillars; Birds will sing in the window, Desolation *will be* on the threshold; For He has laid bare the cedar work.

    C' [15] This is the exultant city Which dwells securely, Who says in her heart, "I am, and there is no one besides me." How **she has become a desolation**, A resting place for beasts! Everyone who passes by her will hiss *And* wave his hand *in contempt.*

Discussion

This chapter starts with an exhortation from the LORD saying that a remnant of Judah, the righteous, will survive the destruction of the nation. The LORD then turns to the enemies of Israel and pronouns judgment.

Questioning the Passage

1. What does it mean to be hidden from the LORD's anger? (v. 3)

   The righteous people of Judah, and those who turn back to the LORD from idol worship before the Day of the LORD, will be spared the LORD's wrath. These people will escape the extinction of all the evil peoples of the world.

2. Where were Gaza, Ashkelon, Ashdod, and Ekron located? (v. 4)

   These cities were located on the coast of the Mediterranean Sea. This territory was the land of the Philistines.

3. Who were the Cherethites? (v. 5)

   Cherethites is another name for the Philistines. They received this name because a province of the Philistine territory was called Cherethi.[7]

4. Why is the seacoast, the land of the Philistines, being given to the remnant of the house of Judah? (v. 7)

   Zephaniah is saying that when the remnant of the LORD's people returns from the Babylonian Exile, they will live on the seacoast.[8]

5. What does it mean to be possessed by nettles and salt pits? (v. 9)

   A land of desolation only has nettles and salt pits growing in it.

[7] Scherman, Nosson, and Meir Zlotowitz.
"Zephaniah." *Isaiah: The Later Prophets with a Commentary Antholigized from the Rabbinic Writings.* Brooklyn, N.Y: Mesorah Publications, 2013. N. pag. Print.
[8] IBID.

Main/Center Point

A very strong warning is issued from the LORD through Zephaniah. The LORD desires to restore His Chosen people and punishing the surrounding nations who assisted in Judah's sacrilege. A remnant of the Hebrew people who turn away from their evil and sin will be saved. The concentration of the chapter focuses on the LORD's judgment against the enemies of Israel. The enemies of Israel are the nations who brought their pagan cults into the land.

Symbols

1. Is there a symbolic reference to the pelican, hedgehog and the other animals noted? (v. 14)

   When the people are removed from the territory, various wild animals can take over the land. The symbolism is that the land will be devoid of people for some time.

Translation Inconsistencies

הִתְקוֹשְׁשׁוּ וָקוֹשּׁוּ הַגּוֹי לֹא נִכְסָף: ^{WTT} Zephaniah 2:1

[NAU] **Zephaniah 2:1** Gather yourselves together, yes, gather, O nation without shame,

[KJV] **Zephaniah 2:1** Gather yourselves together, yea, gather together, O nation not desired;

[LXA] **Zephaniah 2:1** Be ye gathered and closely joined together, O unchastened nation;

[NET] **Zephaniah 2:1** Bunch yourselves together like straw, you undesirable nation,

[NIV] **Zephaniah 2:1** Gather together, gather yourselves together, you shameful nation,

[NRS] **Zephaniah 2:1** Gather together, gather, O shameless nation,

[TNK] **Zephaniah 2:1** Gather together, gather, O nation without shame,

The English word "shame" at the end of the verse in several English versions is inaccurate. The Hebrew word for shame does not appear in this verse. The Targum translation is "Assemble yourselves and come draw near." A good English translation is "Improve yourselves and improve each other, you are a nation without desire." This translation is from the Milstein Edition of the Later Prophets.[9]

Name of places

1. עַזָּה *Azzah* **Meaning:** a Philistine city

2. אַשְׁקְלוֹן *Ashqelon* **Meaning:** a city of the Philistines

3. אַשְׁדּוֹד *Ashdod* **Meaning:** a city of the Philistines

4. עֶקְרוֹן *Eqron* **Meaning:** a Philistine city

5. כְּנַעַן *Kenaan* **Meaning:** a son of Ham, also his descendants and their land west of the Jordan

6. פְּלִשְׁתִּי *Pelishti* **Meaning:** inhabitants of Philistia

7. מוֹאָב *Moab* **Meaning:** a son of Lot, also his desc. and the territory where they settled

8. סְדֹם *Sedom* **Meaning:** a Canaanite city near the Dead Sea

---

[9] Scherman, Nosson, and Meir Zlotowitz. "Zephaniah." *Isaiah: The Later Prophets with a Commentary Antholigized from the Rabbinic Writings.* Brooklyn, N.Y: Mesorah Publications, 2013. N. pag. Print.

9. עֲמֹרָה *Amorah* **Meaning:** a city in the Jordan Valley

10. כּוּשִׁי *Kushi* **Meaning:** descendant of Cush, Ethiopians

11. אַשּׁוּר *Ashshur* **Meaning:** the second son of Shem, also the people of Asshur, also the land of Assyria

12. נִינְוֵה *Nineveh* **Meaning:** capital of Assyria

Thoughts

The usual configuration of a prophetic text is the LORD telling the people about their sins, then about what the wrath of the LORD may look like, and followed by the hope of some survivors. This chapter starts with the LORD telling the people that a remnant of the people would survive. These people will end up living on the coastline of Judah. The coastline was prime land in ancient days. Then the LORD turns toward the enemies of Israel. The nations mentioned had influenced the people of Judah to turn away from their worship of the LORD. They helped to corrupt the people.

What we can learn from this chapter is that we cannot allow anyone to drag us away from our devotion and worship to the LORD. Numerous people who you meet during your life will try to tell you that serving the LORD is a waste of time and resources. What they do not understand is that the LORD's wrath will be upon them. Remaining righteous in the LORD is imperative to receive the blessings of the LORD in this world and the world to come.

Zephaniah Chapter Three

Language

New American Standard 1995	Hebrew	Septuagint
[1] Woe to her who is rebellious and defiled, The tyrannical city! [2] She heeded no voice, She accepted no instruction. She did not trust in the LORD, She did not draw near to her God. [3] Her princes within her are roaring lions, Her judges are wolves at evening; They leave nothing for the morning. [4] Her prophets are reckless, treacherous men; Her priests have profaned the sanctuary. They have done violence to the law. [5] The LORD is righteous within her; He will do no injustice. Every morning He brings His justice to light;	הוֹי מֹרְאָה וְנִגְאָלָה הָעִיר הַיּוֹנָה: [2] לֹא שָׁמְעָה בְּקוֹל לֹא לָקְחָה מוּסָר בַּיהוָה לֹא בָטָחָה אֶל־אֱלֹהֶיהָ לֹא קָרֵבָה: [3] שָׂרֶיהָ בְקִרְבָּה אֲרָיוֹת שֹׁאֲגִים שֹׁפְטֶיהָ זְאֵבֵי עֶרֶב לֹא גָרְמוּ לַבֹּקֶר: [4] נְבִיאֶיהָ פֹּחֲזִים אַנְשֵׁי בֹּגְדוֹת כֹּהֲנֶיהָ חִלְּלוּ־קֹדֶשׁ חָמְסוּ תּוֹרָה: [5] יְהוָה צַדִּיק בְּקִרְבָּה לֹא יַעֲשֶׂה עַוְלָה בַּבֹּקֶר בַּבֹּקֶר מִשְׁפָּטוֹ יִתֵּן לָאוֹר לֹא נֶעְדָּר וְלֹא־יוֹדֵעַ עַוָּל בֹּשֶׁת:	[1] This is the scornful city that dwells securely, that says in her heart, I am, and there is no longer any *to be* after me: how is she become desolate, a habitation of wild beasts! every one that passes through her shall hiss, and shake his hands. Alas the glorious and ransomed city. [2] The dove hearkened not to the voice; she received not correction; she trusted not in the Lord, and she drew not near to her God. [3] Her princes within her were as roaring lions, her judges as the wolves of Arabia; they remained not till the morrow. [4] Her prophets are light *and* scornful

He does not fail. But the unjust knows no shame.

6 "I have cut off nations; Their corner towers are in ruins. I have made their streets desolate, With no one passing by; Their cities are laid waste, Without a man, without an inhabitant.

7 "I said, 'Surely you will revere Me, Accept instruction.' So her dwelling will not be cut off *According to* all that I have appointed concerning her. But they were eager to corrupt all their deeds.

8 "Therefore wait for Me," declares the LORD, "For the day when I rise up as a witness. Indeed, My decision is to gather nations, To assemble kingdoms, To pour out on them My indignation, All My burning anger; For all the earth will be devoured

הִכְרַ֣תִּי גוֹיִ֗ם
נָשַׁ֙מּוּ֙ פִּנּוֹתָ֔ם
הֶחֱרַ֣בְתִּי
חֽוּצוֹתָ֔ם מִבְּלִ֖י
עוֹבֵ֑ר נִצְדּ֧וּ
עָרֵיהֶ֛ם מִבְּלִי־
אִ֖ישׁ מֵאֵ֥ין יוֹשֵֽׁב׃
אָמַ֜רְתִּי אַךְ־
תִּירְאִ֤י אוֹתִי֙
תִּקְחִ֣י מוּסָ֔ר
וְלֹֽא־יִכָּרֵ֣ת
מְעוֹנָ֔הּ כֹּ֥ל
אֲשֶׁר־פָּקַ֖דְתִּי
עָלֶ֑יהָ אָכֵן֙
הִשְׁכִּ֣ימוּ
הִשְׁחִ֔יתוּ כֹּ֖ל
עֲלִילוֹתָֽם׃
לָכֵ֤ן חַכּוּ־לִי֙
נְאֻם־יְהֹוָ֔ה לְי֖וֹם
קוּמִ֣י לְעַ֑ד כִּ֣י
מִשְׁפָּטִי֩ לֶאֱסֹ֨ף
גּוֹיִ֜ם לְקׇבְצִ֣י
מַמְלָכ֗וֹת לִשְׁפֹּ֤ךְ
עֲלֵיהֶם֙ זַעְמִ֔י כֹּ֖ל
חֲר֣וֹן אַפִּ֑י כִּ֠י
בְּאֵ֤שׁ קִנְאָתִי֙
תֵּאָכֵ֣ל כׇּל־
הָאָֽרֶץ׃
כִּֽי־אָ֛ז אֶהְפֹּ֥ךְ
אֶל־עַמִּ֖ים שָׂפָ֣ה
בְרוּרָ֑ה לִקְרֹ֤א
כֻלָּם֙ בְּשֵׁ֣ם יְהֹוָ֔ה

men: her priests profane the holy things, and sinfully transgress the law.

5 But the just Lord is in the midst of her, and he will never do an unjust thing: morning by morning he will bring out his judgment to the light, and it is not hidden, and he knows not injustice by extortion, nor injustice in strife.

6 I have brought down the proud with destruction; their corners are destroyed: I will make their ways completely waste, so that none shall go through: their cities are come to an end, by reason of no man living or dwelling *in them.*

7 I said, But do ye fear me, and receive instruction, and ye shall not be cut off from the face of the land *for* all the vengeance I have brought upon her: prepare thou, rise early: all their produce is spoilt.

By the fire of My zeal.

9 "For then I will give to the peoples purified lips, That all of them may call on the name of the LORD, To serve Him shoulder to shoulder.

10 "From beyond the rivers of Ethiopia My worshipers, My dispersed ones, Will bring My offerings.

11 "In that day you will feel no shame Because of all your deeds By which you have rebelled against Me; For then I will remove from your midst Your proud, exulting ones, And you will never again be haughty On My holy mountain.

12 "But I will leave among you A humble and lowly people, And they will take refuge in the name of the LORD.

13 "The remnant of Israel will do no wrong And tell no

לְעָבְדֹו שְׁכֶם אֶחָֽד׃

10 מֵעֵבֶר לְנַהֲרֵי־כֹוּשׁ עֲתָרַי בַּת־פוּצַי יֹובִלוּן מִנְחָתִֽי׃

11 בַּיֹּום הַהוּא לֹא תֵבֹושִׁי מִכֹּל עֲלִילֹתַיִךְ אֲשֶׁר פָּשַׁעַתְּ בִּי כִּי־אָז ׀ אָסִיר מִקִּרְבֵּךְ עַלִּיזֵי גַּאֲוָתֵךְ וְלֹא־תֹוסִפִי לְגָבְהָה עֹוד בְּהַר קָדְשִֽׁי׃

12 וְהִשְׁאַרְתִּי בְקִרְבֵּךְ עַם עָנִי וָדָל וְחָסוּ בְּשֵׁם יְהוָֽה׃

13 שְׁאֵרִית יִשְׂרָאֵל לֹא־יַעֲשׂוּ עַוְלָה וְלֹא־יְדַבְּרוּ כָזָב וְלֹא־יִמָּצֵא בְּפִיהֶם לְשֹׁון תַּרְמִית כִּי־הֵמָּה יִרְעוּ וְרָבְצוּ וְאֵין מַחֲרִֽיד׃ ס

14 רָנִּי בַּת־צִיֹּון הָרִיעוּ יִשְׂרָאֵל שִׂמְחִי וְעָלְזִי בְּכָל־לֵב בַּת יְרוּשָׁלָֽ͏ִם׃

8 Therefore wait upon me, saith the Lord, until the day when I rise up for a witness: because my judgment *shall be* on the gatherings of the nations, to draw to me kings, to pour out upon them all *my* fierce anger: for the whole earth shall be consumed with the fire of my jealousy.

9 For then will I turn to the peoples a tongue for her generation, that all may call on the name of the Lord, to serve him under one yoke.

10 From the boundaries of the rivers of Ethiopia will I receive my dispersed ones; they shall offer sacrifices to me.

11 In that day thou shalt not be ashamed of all thy practices, wherein thou hast transgressed against me: for then will I take away from thee thy disdainful pride,

lies, Nor will a deceitful tongue Be found in their mouths; For they will feed and lie down With no one to make them tremble."

14 Shout for joy, O daughter of Zion! Shout *in triumph*, O Israel! Rejoice and exult with all *your* heart, O daughter of Jerusalem!

15 The LORD has taken away *His* judgments against you, He has cleared away your enemies. The King of Israel, the LORD, is in your midst; You will fear disaster no more.

16 In that day it will be said to Jerusalem: "Do not be afraid, O Zion; Do not let your hands fall limp.

17 "The LORD your God is in your midst, A victorious warrior. He will exult over you with joy, He will be quiet in His love, He will

---

הֵסִיר יְהוָה 15 מִשְׁפָּטַיִךְ פִּנָּה אֹיְבֵךְ מֶלֶךְ יִשְׂרָאֵל ׀ יְהוָה בְּקִרְבֵּךְ לֹא־ תִירְאִי רָע עוֹד׃ בַּיּוֹם הַהוּא 16 יֵאָמֵר לִירוּשָׁלַם אַל־תִּירָאִי צִיּוֹן אַל־יִרְפּוּ יָדָיִךְ׃ יְהוָה אֱלֹהַיִךְ 17 בְּקִרְבֵּךְ גִּבּוֹר יוֹשִׁיעַ יָשִׂישׂ עָלַיִךְ בְּשִׂמְחָה יַחֲרִישׁ בְּאַהֲבָתוֹ יָגִיל עָלַיִךְ בְּרִנָּה׃ נוּגֵי מִמּוֹעֵד 18 אָסַפְתִּי מִמֵּךְ הָיוּ מַשְׂאֵת עָלֶיהָ חֶרְפָּה׃ הִנְנִי עֹשֶׂה 19 אֶת־כָּל־מְעַנַּיִךְ בָּעֵת הַהִיא וְהוֹשַׁעְתִּי אֶת־ הַצֹּלֵעָה וְהַנִּדָּחָה אֲקַבֵּץ וְשַׂמְתִּים לִתְהִלָּה וּלְשֵׁם בְּכָל־הָאָרֶץ בָּשְׁתָּם׃ בָּעֵת הַהִיא 20 אָבִיא אֶתְכֶם וּבָעֵת קַבְּצִי

---

and thou shalt no more magnify thyself upon my holy mountain.

12 And I will leave in thee a meek and lowly people;

13 and the remnant of Israel shall fear the name of the Lord, and shall do no iniquity, neither shall they speak vanity; neither shall a deceitful tongue be found in their mouth: for they shall feed, and lie down, and there shall be none to terrify them.

14 Rejoice, O daughter of Sion; cry aloud, O daughter of Jerusalem; rejoice and delight thyself with all thine heart, O daughter of Jerusalem.

15 The Lord has taken away thine iniquities, he has ransomed thee from the hand of thine enemies: the Lord, the King of Israel, is in the midst of thee: thou shalt not see evil any more.

rejoice over you with shouts of joy.

18 "I will gather those who grieve about the appointed feasts-- They came from you, *O Zion*; *The* reproach *of exile* is a burden on them.

19 "Behold, I am going to deal at that time With all your oppressors, I will save the lame And gather the outcast, And I will turn their shame into praise and renown In all the earth.

20 "At that time I will bring you in, Even at the time when I gather you together; Indeed, I will give you renown and praise Among all the peoples of the earth, When I restore your fortunes before your eyes," Says the LORD.

אֶתְכֶם כִּי־אֶתֵּן אֶתְכֶם לְשֵׁם וְלִתְהִלָּה בְּכֹל עַמֵּי הָאָרֶץ בְּשׁוּבִי אֶת־ שְׁבוּתֵיכֶם לְעֵינֵיכֶם אָמַר יְהוָה׃

16 At that time the Lord shall say to Jerusalem, Be of good courage, Sion; let not thine hands be slack.

17 The Lord thy God is in thee; the Mighty One shall save thee: he shall bring joy upon thee, and shall refresh thee with his love; and he shall rejoice over thee with delight as in a day of feasting.

18 And I will gather thine afflicted ones. Alas! who has taken up a reproach against her?

19 Behold, I *will* work in thee for thy sake at that time, saith the Lord: and I will save her that was oppressed, and receive her that was rejected; and I will make them a praise, and honoured in all the earth.

20 And *their enemies* shall be ashamed at that time, when I shall deal well with you, and at the time

		when I shall receive you: for I will make you honoured and a praise among all the nations of the earth, when I turn back your captivity before you, saith the Lord.

Process of Discovery

Linguistics Section

Linguistic Structure

A [1] Woe to her who is rebellious and defiled, The tyrannical city! [2] She heeded no voice, She accepted no instruction. She did not trust in the LORD, She did not draw near to her God. [3] Her princes within her are roaring lions, Her judges are wolves at evening; They leave nothing for the morning. [4] Her prophets are reckless, treacherous men; Her priests have profaned the sanctuary. They have done violence to the law. [5] The LORD is righteous within her; **He will do no injustice**. Every morning He brings His justice to light; He does not fail. But the unjust knows no shame.

B [6] "I have cut off nations; Their corner towers are in ruins. I have made their streets desolate, With no one passing by; Their cities are laid waste, Without a man, without an inhabitant. **[Cause]**

C [7] "I said, 'Surely you will revere Me, Accept instruction.' So her dwelling will not be cut off *According to* all that I have appointed concerning her. But they were eager to corrupt all their deeds. [8] "Therefore wait for Me," declares the LORD, "For the day when I rise up as a witness. Indeed, My decision is to gather nations, To assemble kingdoms, To pour out on them My indignation, All My burning anger; For all the earth will be devoured By the fire of My zeal.

B' [9] "For then I will give to the peoples purified lips, That all of them may call on the name of the

LORD, To serve Him shoulder to shoulder. [10] "From beyond the rivers of Ethiopia My worshipers, My dispersed ones, Will bring My offerings. **[Effect]**

A' [11] "In that day you will feel no shame Because of all your deeds By which you have rebelled against Me; For then I will remove from your midst Your proud, exulting ones, And you will never again be haughty On My holy mountain. [12] "But I will leave among you A humble and lowly people, And they will take refuge in the name of the LORD. [13] **"The remnant of Israel will do no wrong And tell no lies**, Nor will a deceitful tongue Be found in their mouths; For they will feed and lie down With no one to make them tremble."

A [14] Shout for joy, O daughter of Zion! Shout *in triumph*, O Israel! Rejoice and exult with all *your* heart, O daughter of Jerusalem! [15] The LORD has taken away *His* judgments against you, **He has cleared away your enemies.** The King of Israel, the LORD, is in your midst; You will fear disaster no more. [16] In that day it will be said to Jerusalem: "Do not be afraid, O Zion; Do not let your hands fall limp. [17] "The LORD your God is in your midst, A victorious warrior. He will exult over you with joy, He will be quiet in His love, He will rejoice over you with shouts of joy.

B [18] "I will gather those who grieve about the appointed feasts-- They came from you, *O Zion; The* reproach *of exile* is a burden on them.
A' [19] "Behold, **I am going to deal at that time With all your oppressors,** I will save the lame And gather the outcast, And I will turn their shame into praise and

renown In all the earth.[20] "At that time I will bring you in, Even at the time when I gather you together; Indeed, I will give you renown and praise Among all the peoples of the earth, When I restore your fortunes before your eyes," Says the LORD.

Discussion

This chapter has two chiasms. The first chiasm deals with the godlessness that was occurring in Jerusalem. The second chiasm gives the people the hope of their restoration and the destruction of all the nations which influenced Judah into sin.

Questioning the Passage

1. Which city is the LORD referring to in verse one?

    The LORD refers to the city of Jerusalem.[10]

1. Why are the princes likened to roaring lions? (v. 3)

    The princes and royalty of Jerusalem were terrifying the people to follow them to serve the

---

[10] IBID.

pagan gods. They were as terrifying as roaring lions.[11]

2. Why are the judges likened to wolves in the evening? (v. 3)

   The judges of the city took bribe therefore, justice was not being given to the common and poor people. The judges are thought to consume their ill-gotten gains as quickly as they received them. Wolves in the evening will attack small animals and consume them before daybreak.[12] Many court cases where occurring at night.

3. Who are the nations described in verse six?

   The nations are all of Judah's enemies.

4. What does it mean to receive purified lips from the LORD? (v. 9)

   The Targum reads the LORD will bring one language to the nations of the Earth. Therefore, purified lips could be understood as all the

---

[11] IBID.
[12] IBID.

nations and people of the world speaking God's language, that is Hebrew.

Main/Center Point

The city of Jerusalem is being called out for her sins against the LORD. The people of Jerusalem needed to be reminded that they were in violation of the Torah as much as the nations that surrounded them. They would also have to suffer a punishment at the hands of the LORD. The hope of restoration for the LORD's people is repeated. After the punishment has been upon them for some undisclosed time, the LORD was going to lift the punishment and restore the remnant of the people.

Name of places

1. צִיּוֹן *Tsiyyon* **Meaning:** a mountain in Jer., also a name for Jerusalem

2. יְרוּשָׁלַם *Yerushalaim* or יְרוּשָׁלַיִם *Yerushalayim* **Meaning:** prob. 'foundation of peace,' capital city of all Israel

Thoughts

The third chapter of Zephaniah gives a strong condemnation for Jerusalem. Perhaps the Hebrew people felt they were immune to the wrath of the LORD because they were the Chosen people. I cannot believe this because they saw the destruction of the Northern Kingdom. However, several Southern Kingdom writings show the North deserved being destroyed for violating the Torah. Yeshua said that one should not discuss the stick in another person's eye when a log was on their own. The warning to us is that we must not look at what others are doing or not doing for the LORD, but look at ourselves.

I have seen in Yeshua's churches people who look at other members of the congregation making comments about how they live and what they contribute to the LORD. Then you discover what the complainers really contribute and do for Yeshua's church. These complainers tend to act righteous and all the time they are worse than the people they are condemning. When you attend worship to the LORD, you should because you want to do it. You give to the LORD what the

LORD requires, not what the congregation or pastor says.

The people of Jerusalem discovered too late that they handled their misbehavior. The people of God today must learn the same lesson.

Bibliography

Errico, Rocco A. 2012. *Aramaic Light on Ezekiel, Daniel and the Minor Prophets.* Smyrna, GA: Noohra Foundation.

Scherman, Noson, and Meir Zlotowitz. 203. *Isaiah: The later prophets with a commentary.* Brooklyn, NY: Mesorah Publications.

www.ingramcontent.com/pod-product-compliance
Lightning Source LLC
Chambersburg PA
CBHW060459160726
47992CB00003B/1246